Freya zoe siti on

I say

The Jacqueline Wilson Daydream Journal

Illustrated by Nick Sharratt

DOUBLEDAY

Jacqueline Wilson loved reading and writing stories as a child. She was a little girl with a very vivid imagination, and losing herself in a new world was the best possible way she could spend time.

In this extract from *Jacky Daydream*, you can see her mother giving her advice on her first day at Latchmere Infants school!

'You must look both ways every time you cross a road, do you hear me?' said Biddy.
'Yes, Mummy.'
'There's a traffic lady at the Park Road crossroads – she'll show you across.'
'Yes, Mummy.'
'You do know the way by now, don't you Jac?'
'Yes, Mummy.'
'And you won't ever talk to any strange men?'
'Yes, Mummy.'
'What?'
'I mean, no, Mummy.'
'And absolutely no daydreaming!'
'Yes, Mummy. No, Mummy,' I said. No daydreaming! It was as if she was telling me to stop breathing.

When Jacqueline was a little older, in the top juniors, her teacher was called Mr Branson. He was a fierce teacher who was often cross with his class — and he wasn't very patient with Jacqueline, as she tells us here.

If you settled into a little daydream, he'd aim his sharpened chalk at you with surprising accuracy, so that it really stung. If you were ever unwise enough to yawn, you had to run round the playground five times to get some oxygen into your lungs. He urged you to go 'Faster! Faster!' until your lungs weren't just freshly oxygenated, they were in danger of total collapse. We might not have called him nicknames to his face, but he had plenty for us, mostly unpleasant. I managed to be Top Girl, in spite of my lamentable maths, so I think he quite liked me. In fond moods he'd call me Jacky Daydream, almost a term of endearment for Mr Branson.

Tracy Beaker's Hopes and Dreams

When I'm older, I'm going to live in this really great modern house all on my own, and I'd have my own 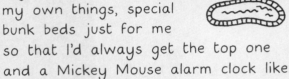 huge bedroom with all  my own things, special bunk beds just for me so that I'd always get the top one and a Mickey Mouse alarm clock like Justine's and my own giant set of poster paints and I'd have some felt tips as well and no-one would  ever get to borrow them and mess them up and I'd have my own television and choose exactly what programmes I want, and I'd stay up till gone twelve every night  and I'd eat at McDonald's every single day and I'd 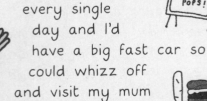 have a big fast car so I could whizz off and visit my mum whenever I wanted.

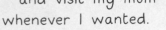

Tracy Beaker's Hopes and Dreams

When I grow up I am going to be
a world famous actress, like my mum.

I'm going to be on the telly with my own chat
show – The Tracy Beaker Experience. I'd walk out
on to this stage in a sparkly dress and all the
studio audience would clap and cheer and all these
famous celebrities would fight tooth and nail to
get on my show to speak to me.

Tracy Beaker's Hopes and Dreams

I reckon I could write books, too. I've always been absolutely Tip Top at writing stories, but since I've been at this stupid new school Mrs Vomit Bagley just puts *'Disgracefully untidy work, Tracy'* and *'Check your spellings!'*

These are my favourite animals to illustrate.

These are all things I've found it useful to know how to draw. It's funny how often they crop up in my work!

An interview with
NICK SHARRATT

By Ruby and Garnet

Hello, Mr Sharratt. How long have you been an illustrator?

Please, call me Nick. I've been a full-time illustrator ever since I finished art school, which was over twenty years ago.

Wow! You must be really old now.

Ruby! Shhh! You can't say things like that.

Sorry, Nick. I know you're not old, not like Gran, not even like our dad. So, where did you go to art school?

First of all I did a foundation course in Manchester and then I went to London and studied at the St Martin's School of Art.

Did you always know you wanted to be an illustrator?

Even at primary school I was sure that I wanted to do something that involved art, and once I discovered illustration and graphic design I knew I'd found the perfect work for me.

Yes, I think that if you're born being really good at something you know you could do it for a living, don't you? It's like me and acting. It's just a shame Garnet got all nervous and silly at that audition we went to, otherwise we'd probably be famous actresses on telly by now.

Speak for yourself, Ruby. On second thoughts, it might be better if you spoke a bit less. We're supposed to be finding out about Nick Sharratt and all his pictures that are in Jacqueline Wilson's books.

Is that all you do, Nick? Just draw the pictures for Jacqueline's books?

With two new novels a year needing covers and inside artwork, plus the Jacqueline Wilson Diary and various other extra Jacky books, that keeps me busy, but no, I do lots of other work as well. Some of the things are connected with my work on Jacky's books. For example, I help with the animations for the Tracy Beaker TV series and check how my artwork is being used on merchandise such as Jacqueline Wilson pencil cases and so on. But I also illustrate picture books for younger children, such as the hilarious stories about Daisy by Kes Gray and Pants by Giles Andreae. I also write and illustrate my own picture books, like Shark in the Park, Ketchup on Your Cornflakes and Don't Put Your Finger in the Jelly, Nelly.

Have you been working with Jacqueline for a long time?

Yes, actually, for more than fifteen years now. The first book of hers that I illustrated was The Story of Tracy

Beaker, which was published in 1991, and there have been another 33 novels since then.

Gosh, don't you ever get fed up with each other?

No, we're good friends and always enjoy getting together when we have the chance.

Oh, I thought you probably lived in the same house . . .

Don't be silly, Ruby . . .

Actually, no, but lots of people think that. I live in Brighton on the south coast and Jacky lives in Kingston, in Surrey.

Do you work at home?

Yes, I have a studio at the top of my house. The seagulls peer through the window and watch me at my desk.

Do you work on one book at a time?

No, I have lots of projects on the go at the same time and I hardly ever spend the whole day working on just one book. I use the mornings for 'thinking' work: coming up with ideas and doing rough sketches. In the afternoon I usually do final artwork. I draw my black and white pictures in soft pencil or with a technical pen. I used to use charcoal and watercolour inks but now I do nearly all my colouring on my computer.

So are you stuck in your studio every day?

No, not every single day. I often have to go to London for meetings with publishers. I also sometimes do events for children at literary festivals and I've visited lots of schools over the years.

You're so busy. Do you ever get any time off?

Not much!

Do you ever get to have a holiday?

Yes, I have two or three lovely holidays a year and when I'm on holiday I don't do any drawing at all!

We were wondering where you get your ideas from? How do you decide what characters should look like?

Do you just stick to what Jacqueline says in the story?

I read the story very carefully and by the time I've finished it I've picked up enough clues to imagine how the author sees the characters.

Thanks, Nick. It's been great talking to you.

Yeah, thanks very much. Perhaps we'll have a go at illustrating our story in our Accounts book now.

1 JANUARY

Nothing Love

Realy Just LUV

Lu Drawing !! Luv

Love rove

Love Luv

2 JANUARY

Pasx LOL

DaviD's

AVOS

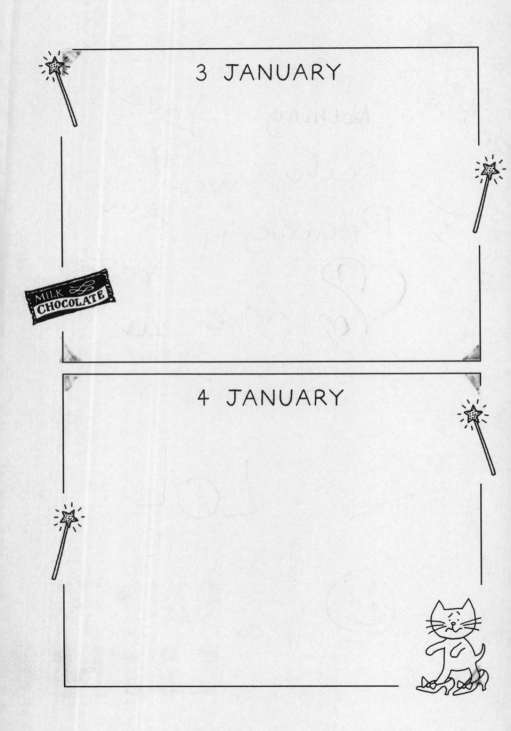

3 JANUARY

4 JANUARY

5 JANUARY

6 JANUARY

Tia faz anos

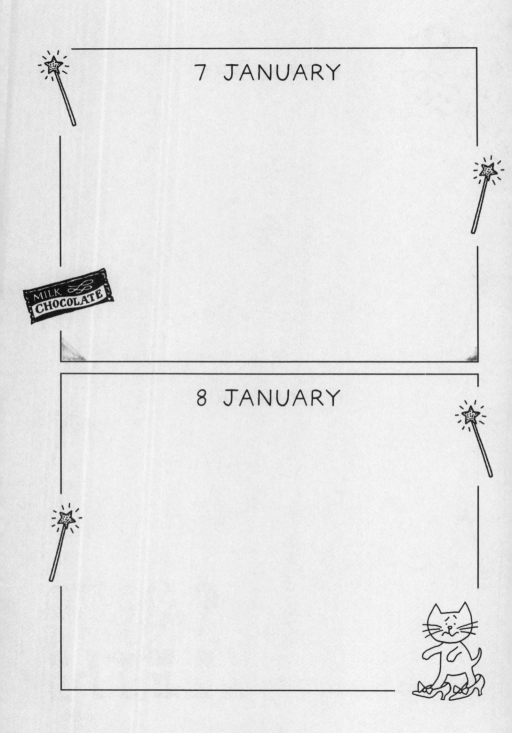

7 JANUARY

8 JANUARY

9 JANUARY

10 JANUARY

11 JANUARY

12 JANUARY

13 JANUARY

14 JANUARY

15 JANUARY

16 JANUARY

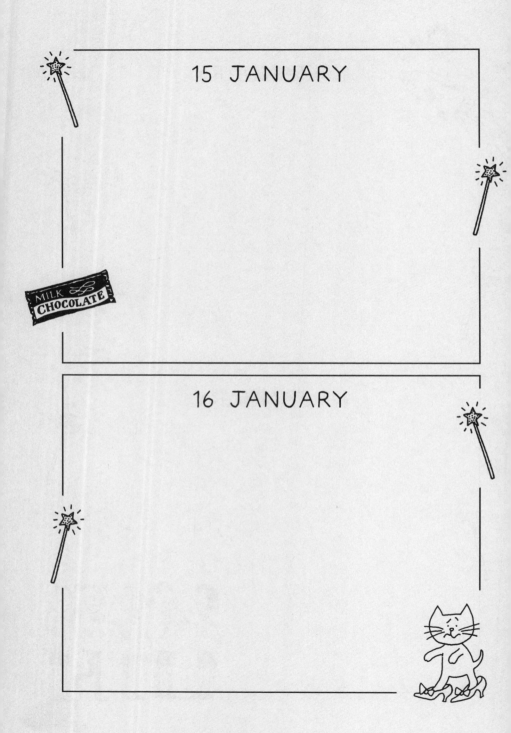

17 JANUARY

18 JANUARY

19 JANUARY

20 JANUARY

21 JANUARY

22 JANUARY

23 JANUARY

24 JANUARY

25 JANUARY

26 JANUARY

27 JANUARY

28 JANUARY

29 JANUARY

30 JANUARY

31 JANUARY

1 FEBRUARY

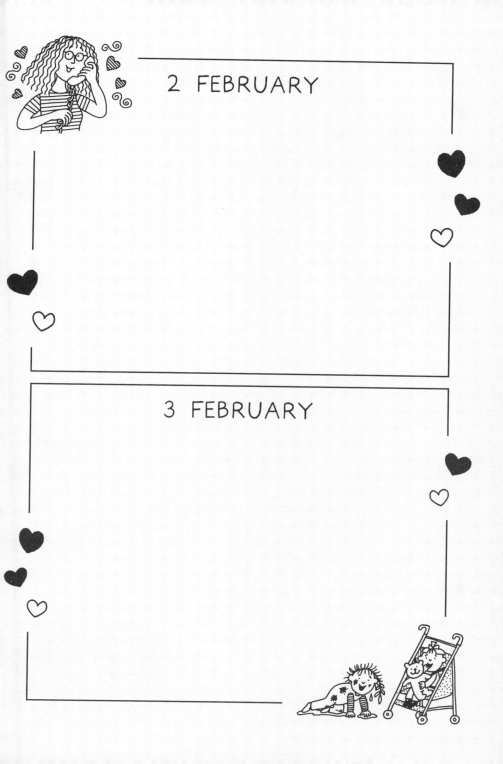

2 FEBRUARY

3 FEBRUARY

4 FEBRUARY

5 FEBRUARY

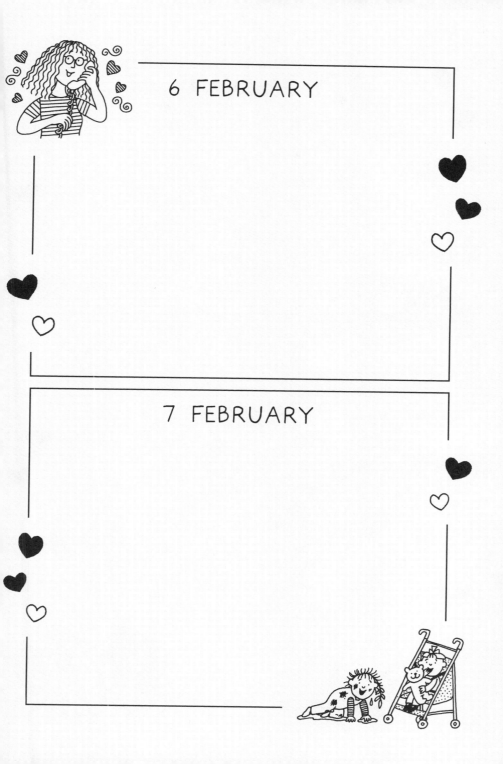

6 FEBRUARY

7 FEBRUARY

8 FEBRUARY

9 FEBRUARY

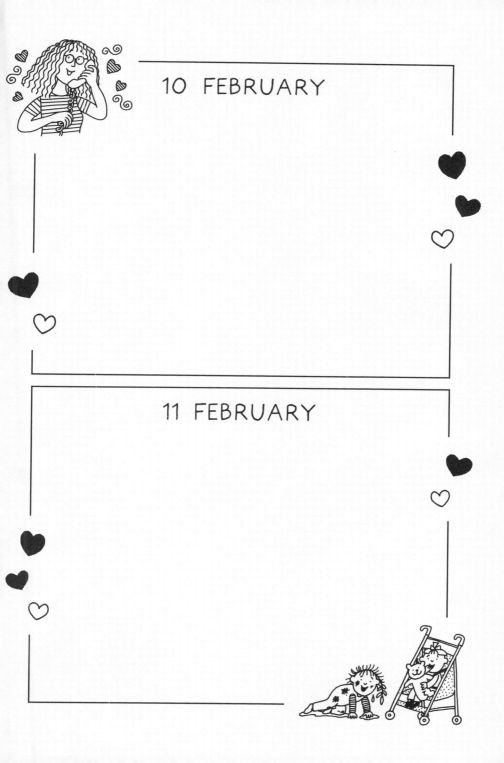

10 FEBRUARY

11 FEBRUARY

12 FEBRUARY

13 FEBRUARY

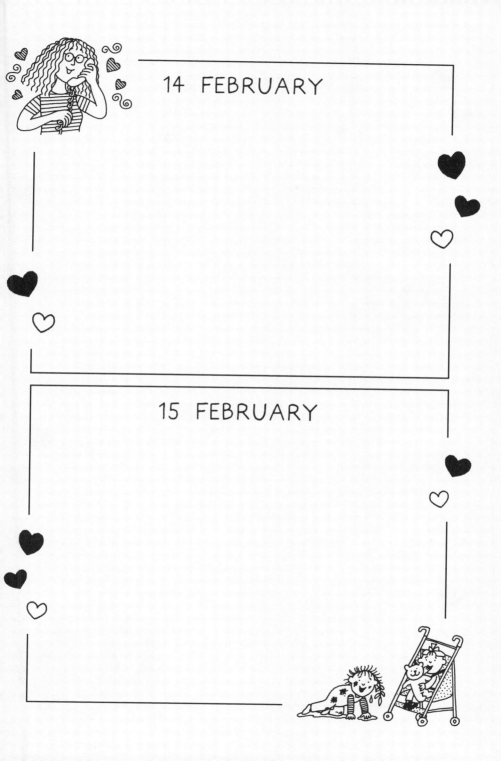

14 FEBRUARY

15 FEBRUARY

16 FEBRUARY

17 FEBRUARY

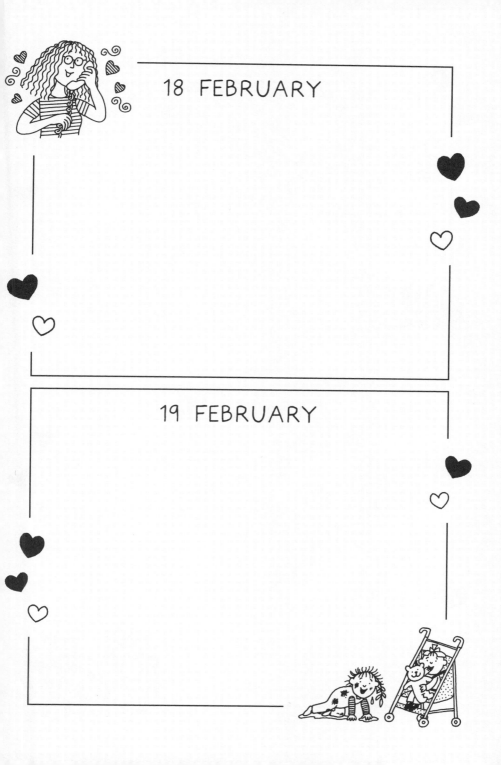

18 FEBRUARY

19 FEBRUARY

20 FEBRUARY

21 FEBRUARY

22 FEBRUARY

23 FEBRUARY

24 FEBRUARY

25 FEBRUARY

26 FEBRUARY

27 FEBRUARY

28 FEBRUARY

29 FEBRUARY
Leap year only

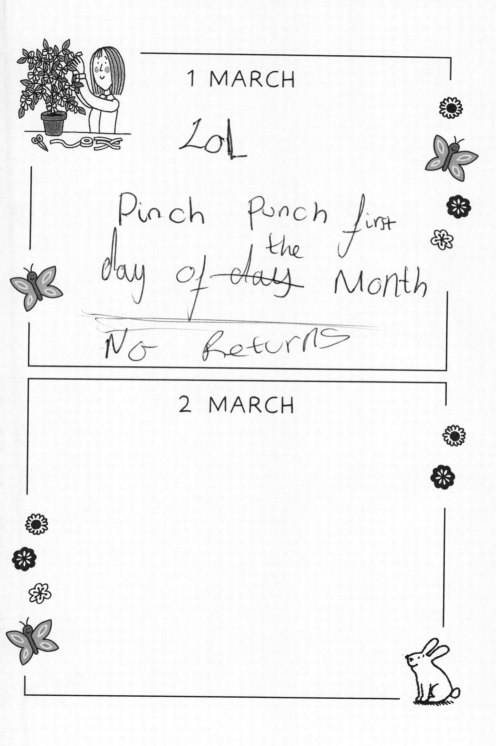

1 MARCH

LoL

Pinch Punch first
day of ~~day~~ the Month

No Returns

2 MARCH

3 MARCH

4 MARCH

Patrina's B-day

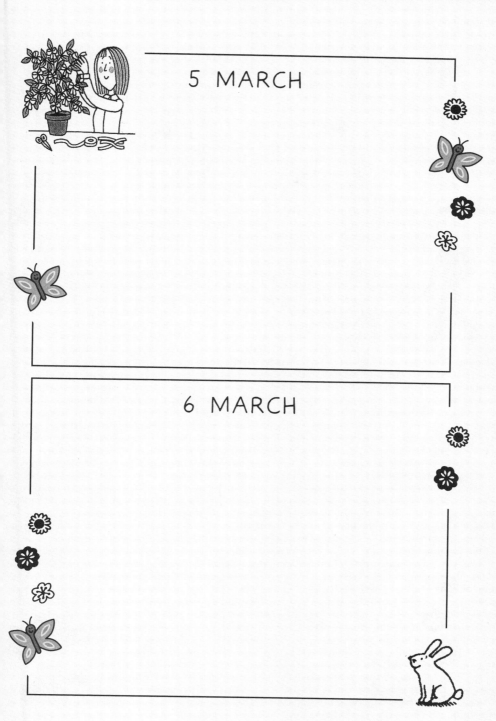

5 MARCH

6 MARCH

7 MARCH

8 MARCH

9 MARCH

Issabel10 MARCH

BFF's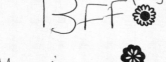

Grace gave Me Magic Powers!!!

11 MARCH

12 MARCH

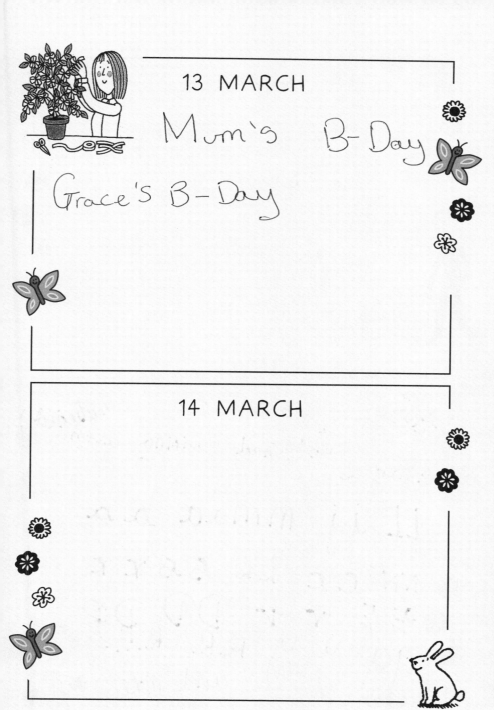

13 MARCH

Mum's B-Day

Grace's B-Day

14 MARCH

15 MARCH

16 MARCH

Spell
ing

handwriting

Jus' had writing with
year 2.

ff jj mmaa aa
NN cc hh ss xx
EE rr DD PP
gg yy RR R....
and more

17 MARCH

lauren says happy B-Day to my dad

Dads B-Day

I sabelle and grace make a secret

18 MARCH

Red nose day dress in Red bring in funny glasses and practice with chloe Freya zoe Some thing funny for money

19 MARCH

20 MARCH

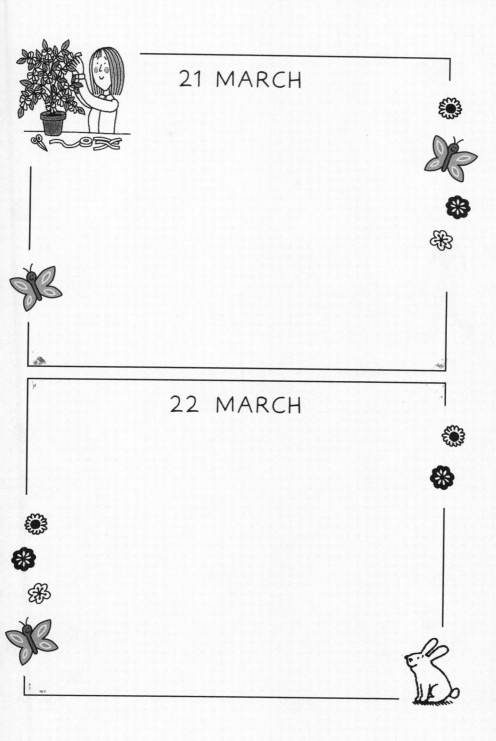

21 MARCH

22 MARCH

23 MARCH

24 MARCH

25 MARCH

26 MARCH

27 MARCH

28 MARCH

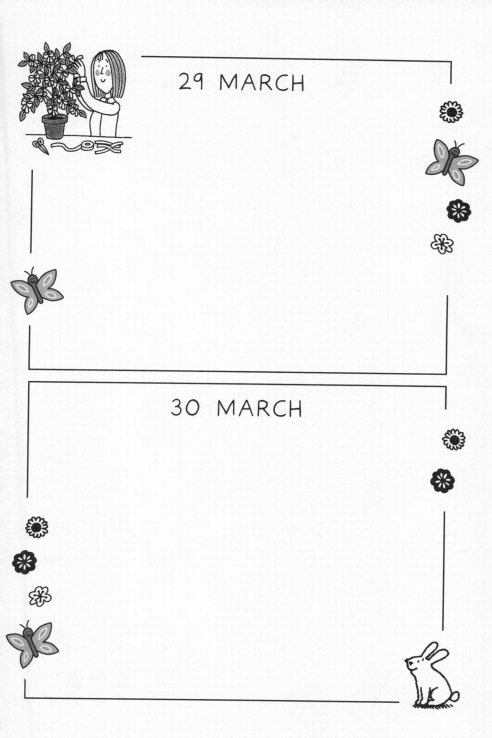

29 MARCH

30 MARCH

31 MARCH

1 APRIL

2 APRIL

3 APRIL

4 APRIL

5 APRIL

6 APRIL

7 APRIL

8 APRIL

9 APRIL

10 APRIL

11 APRIL

12 APRIL

13 APRIL

14 APRIL

15 APRIL

16 APRIL

17 APRIL

18 APRIL

19 APRIL

20 APRIL

21 APRIL

22 APRIL

23 APRIL

24 APRIL

25 APRIL

26 APRIL

27 APRIL

28 APRIL

29 APRIL

30 APRIL

1 MAY

2 MAY

3 MAY

4 MAY

5 MAY

6 MAY

7 MAY

8 MAY

May fair take
Macy if she cant go
Isabelle if she cant go
Grace

9 MAY

10 MAY

My Luv came true

11 MAY

12 MAY

13 MAY

14 MAY

15 MAY

16 MAY

17 MAY

18 MAY

19 MAY

20 MAY

21 MAY

22 MAY

23 MAY

24 MAY

25 MAY

26 MAY

27 MAY

28 MAY

29 MAY

30 MAY

31 MAY

1 JUNE

2 JUNE

3 JUNE

4 JUNE

5 JUNE

6 JUNE

7 JUNE

8 JUNE

9 JUNE

10 JUNE

11 JUNE

12 JUNE

13 JUNE

14 JUNE

15 JUNE

Grandad's B-Day

16 JUNE

17 JUNE

18 JUNE

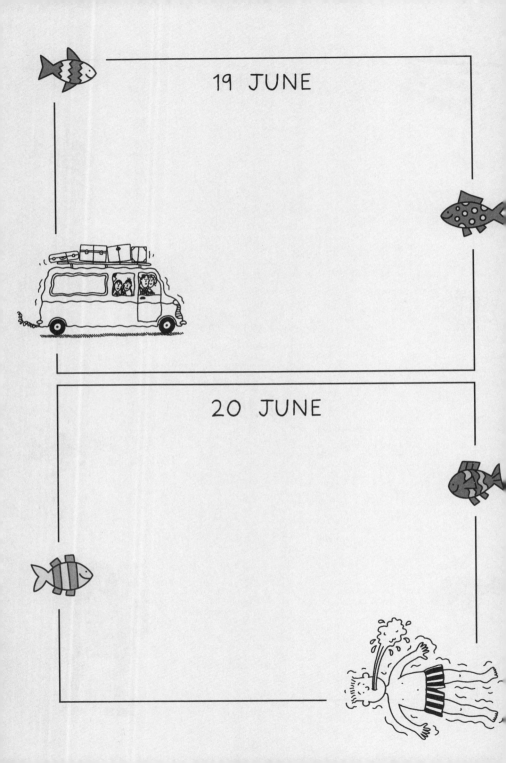

19 JUNE

20 JUNE

21 JUNE

22 JUNE

23 JUNE

24 JUNE

25 JUNE

26 JUNE

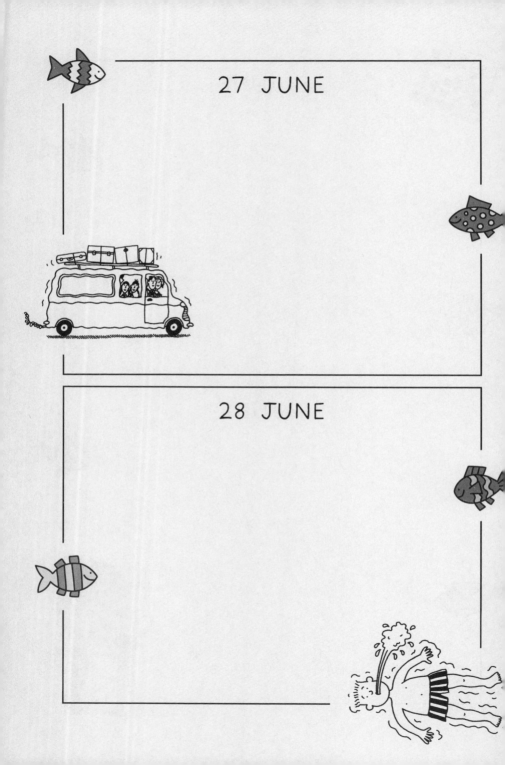

27 JUNE

28 JUNE

29 JUNE

30 JUNE

1 JULY

2 JULY

3 JULY

4 JULY

5 JULY

6 JULY

7 JULY

8 JULY

9 JULY

10 JULY

11 JULY

12 JULY

13 JULY

14 JULY

15 JULY

16 JULY

17 JULY

18 JULY

19 JULY

20 JULY

21 JULY

22 JULY

23 JULY

24 JULY

25 JULY

26 JULY

27 JULY

28 JULY

29 JULY

30 JULY

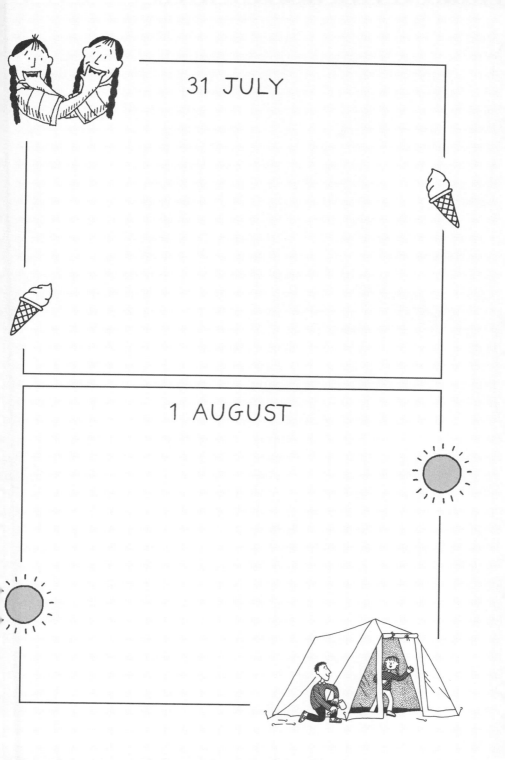

31 JULY

1 AUGUST

2 AUGUST

3 AUGUST

4 AUGUST

5 AUGUST

6 AUGUST

7 AUGUST

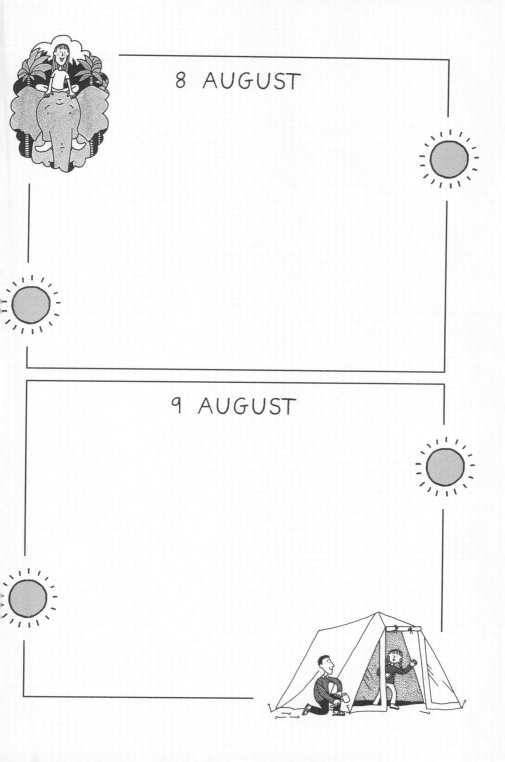

8 AUGUST

9 AUGUST

10 AUGUST

11 AUGUST

12 AUGUST

13 AUGUST

14 AUGUST

15 AUGUST

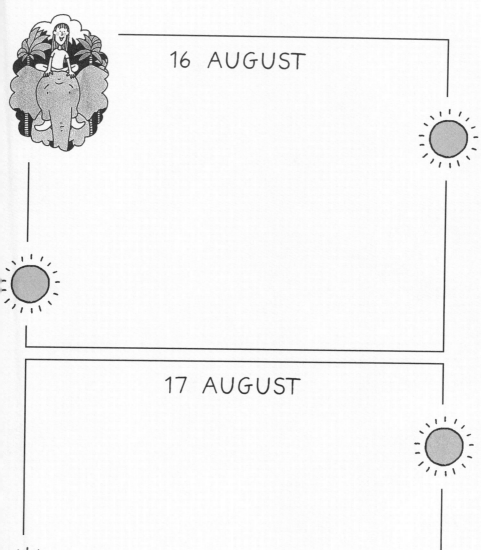

16 AUGUST

17 AUGUST

18 AUGUST

19 AUGUST

20 AUGUST

21 AUGUST

22 AUGUST

23 AUGUST

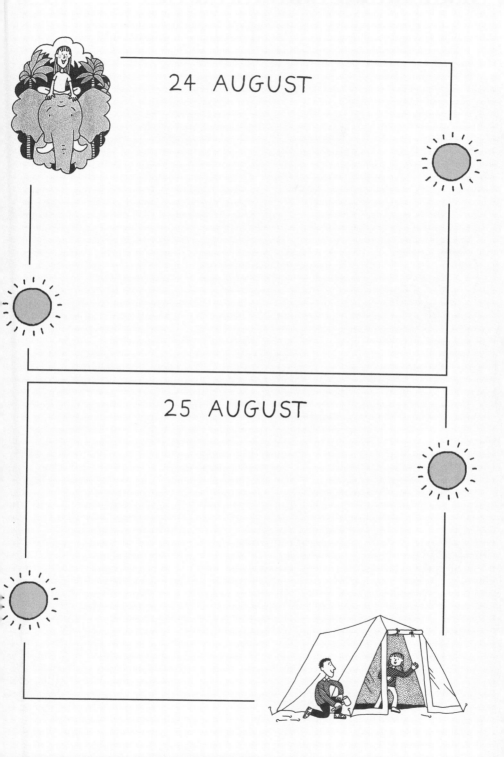

24 AUGUST

25 AUGUST

26 AUGUST

27 AUGUST

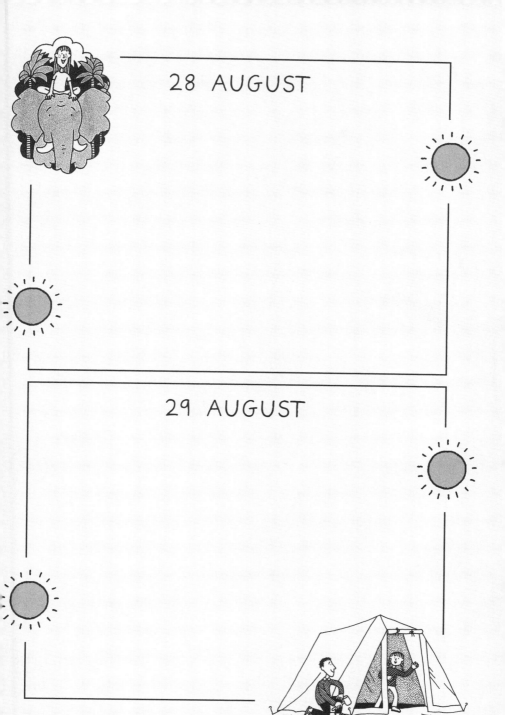

28 AUGUST

29 AUGUST

30 AUGUST

31 AUGUST

1 SEPTEMBER

2 SEPTEMBER

3 SEPTEMBER

4 SEPTEMBER

5 SEPTEMBER

6 SEPTEMBER

7 SEPTEMBER

8 SEPTEMBER

9 SEPTEMBER

10 SEPTEMBER

11 SEPTEMBER

12 SEPTEMBER

13 SEPTEMBER

14 SEPTEMBER

Today I woce UP
Late. Then I
We

15 SEPTEMBER

16 SEPTEMBER

17 SEPTEMBER

18 SEPTEMBER

19 SEPTEMBER

20 SEPTEMBER

21 SEPTEMBER

22 SEPTEMBER

23 SEPTEMBER

24 SEPTEMBER

25 SEPTEMBER

26 SEPTEMBER

27 SEPTEMBER

28 SEPTEMBER

29 SEPTEMBER

30 SEPTEMBER

1 OCTOBER

2 OCTOBER

3 OCTOBER

4 OCTOBER

5 OCTOBER

6 OCTOBER

7 OCTOBER

8 OCTOBER

9 OCTOBER

10 OCTOBER

11 OCTOBER

12 OCTOBER

13 OCTOBER

14 OCTOBER

15 OCTOBER

16 OCTOBER

17 OCTOBER

18 OCTOBER

19 OCTOBER

20 OCTOBER

21 OCTOBER

22 OCTOBER

23 OCTOBER

24 OCTOBER

25 OCTOBER

26 OCTOBER

27 OCTOBER

28 OCTOBER

29 OCTOBER

30 OCTOBER

31 OCTOBER

1 NOVEMBER

2 NOVEMBER

3 NOVEMBER

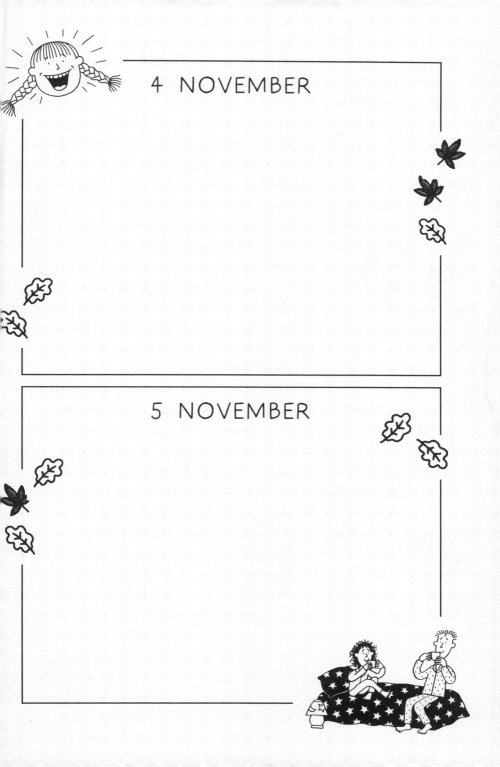

4 NOVEMBER

5 NOVEMBER

6 NOVEMBER

7 NOVEMBER

Lauren's B-Day

8 NOVEMBER

9 NOVEMBER

10 NOVEMBER

11 NOVEMBER

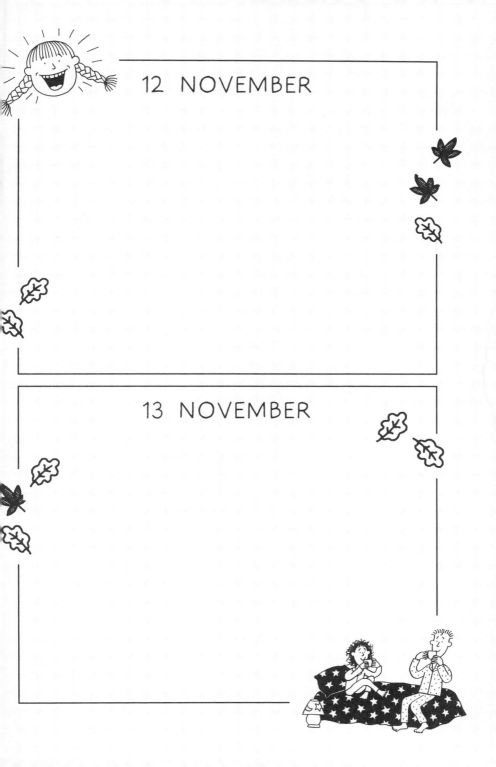

12 NOVEMBER

13 NOVEMBER

14 NOVEMBER

15 NOVEMBER

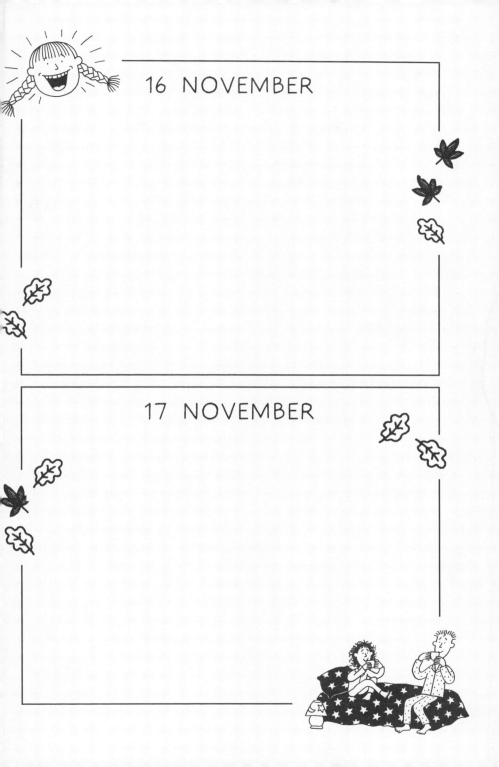

16 NOVEMBER

17 NOVEMBER

18 NOVEMBER

19 NOVEMBER

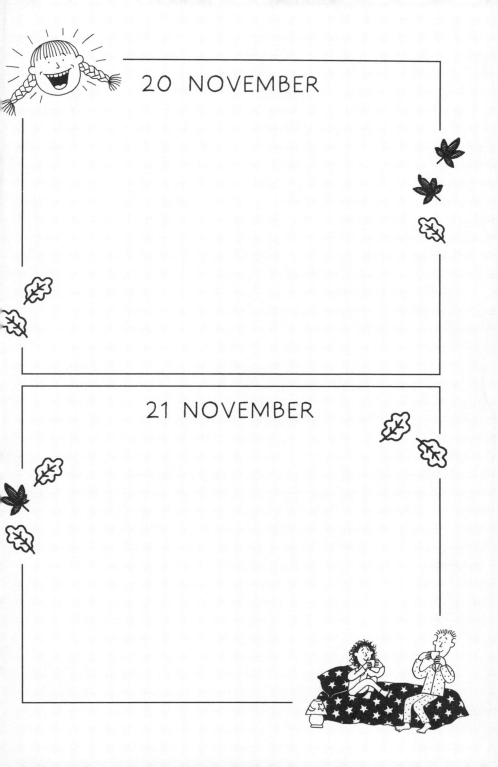

20 NOVEMBER

21 NOVEMBER

22 NOVEMBER

23 NOVEMBER

24 NOVEMBER

Grandma's B-Day

25 NOVEMBER

My B-Day

26 NOVEMBER

27 NOVEMBER

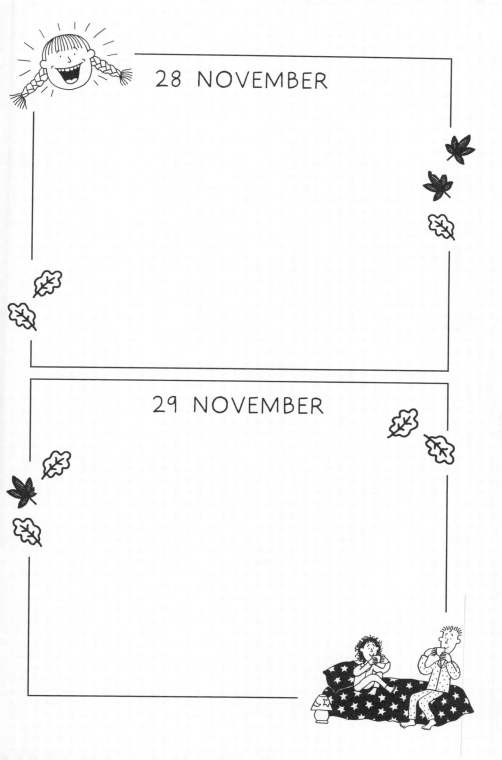

28 NOVEMBER

29 NOVEMBER

30 NOVEMBER

1 DECEMBER

2 DECEMBER

3 DECEMBER

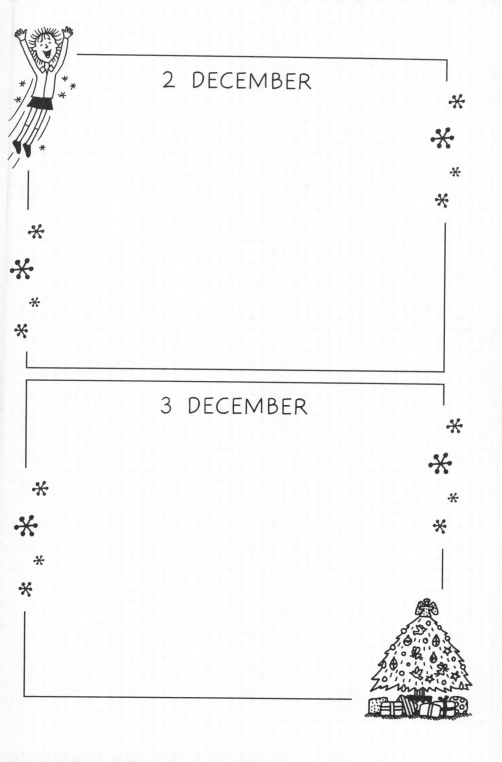

4 DECEMBER

5 DECEMBER

6 DECEMBER

7 DECEMBER

8 DECEMBER

9 DECEMBER

10 DECEMBER

11 DECEMBER

12 DECEMBER

13 DECEMBER

14 DECEMBER

15 DECEMBER

16 DECEMBER

17 DECEMBER

18 DECEMBER

19 DECEMBER

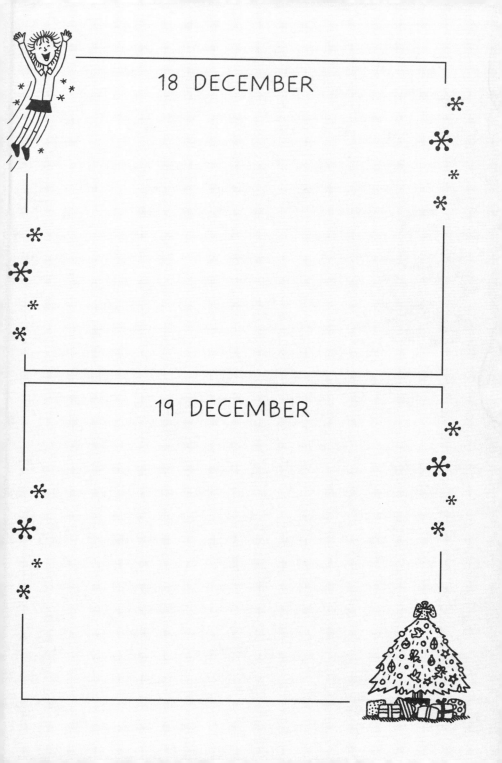

20 DECEMBER

21 DECEMBER

22 DECEMBER

23 DECEMBER

24 DECEMBER

25 DECEMBER

26 DECEMBER

27 DECEMBER

28 DECEMBER

29 DECEMBER

30 DECEMBER

31 DECEMBER

JACKY DAYDREAM

THE STORY OF HER CHILDHOOD

Everybody knows Tracy Beaker, Jacqueline Wilson's best-loved character. But what do they know about the little girl who grew up to become Jacqueline Wilson?

How she played with paper dolls like April in *Dustbin Baby*.

How she dealt with an unpredictable father like Prue in *Love Lessons*.

How she chose new toys in Hamleys like Dolphin in *The Illustrated Mum*.

How she enjoyed Christmas like Em in *Clean Break*.

How she sat entrance exams like Ruby in *Double Act*.

But most of all how she loved reading and writing stories. Losing herself in a new world was the best possible way she could think of spending her time. From the very first story she wrote, *Meet the Maggots*, it was clear that this little girl had a very vivid imagination. But who would've guessed that she would grow up to be the mega-bestselling, award-winning Jacqueline Wilson!

Illustrated by Nick Sharratt

MY SECRET DIARY

JACQUELINE WILSON

Dating, Dancing, Dreams and Dilemmas!
Includes extracts from Jacqueline's real diary!

'Saw my Ken again this morning. Sue can't understand what I see in him as he isn't really handsome. I don't know what it is myself, except that I like him so much'

In 1960, you'd wear stiff petticoats and dancing shoes. Now, you'd wear jeans and trainers.

In 1960, you'd spend hours listening to records in your local store. Now, you'd spend hours listening to music online.

In 1960 you'd learn all the steps to the latest dances. Now, you just make up your own moves.

But girls always have and always will have crushes on boys, argue with their parents, get embarrassed at school, want to stay out with their friends, and spend hours fixing their hair . . .

A wonderfully written and engaging memoir of life as a teenager. Includes original photos of Jacqueline and her friends.

Illustrated by Nick Sharratt

MY SISTER JODIE
SECRETS
STARRING TRACY BEAKER
THE STORY OF TRACY BEAKER
THE SUITCASE KID
VICKY ANGEL
THE WORRY WEBSITE

COLLECTIONS:
THE JACQUELINE WILSON COLLECTION
includes THE STORY OF TRACY BEAKER
and THE BED AND BREAKFAST STAR
JACQUELINE WILSON'S DOUBLE-DECKER
includes BAD GIRLS *and* DOUBLE ACT
JACQUELINE WILSON'S SUPERSTARS
includes THE SUITCASE KID *and*
THE LOTTIE PROJECT

AVAILABLE FROM DOUBLEDAY/CORGI BOOKS,
FOR OLDER READERS:
DUSTBIN BABY
GIRLS IN LOVE
GIRLS UNDER PRESSURE
GIRLS OUT LATE
GIRLS IN TEARS
KISS
LOLA ROSE
LOVE LESSONS

Join the official Jacqueline Wilson fan club
at www.jacquelinewilson.co.uk

Join the FREE online

Jacqueline Wilson

☆ FAN CLUB ☆

Read Jacqueline's diary, submit questions
to her, receive e-newsletters and
check tour info.

Plus, quizzes, jokes, photos to download,
a fabulous members' message board
and loads more.

www.jacquelinewilson.co.uk

THE JACQUELINE WILSON DAYDREAM JOURNAL
A DOUBLEDAY BOOK 978 0 385 61715 4

Published in Great Britain by Doubleday,
an imprint of Random House Children's Books
A Random House Group Company

This edition published 2009

1 3 5 7 9 10 8 6 4 2

The Random House Group Limited supports the Forest Stewardship
Council (FSC), the leading international forest certification organization.
All our titles that are printed on Greenpeace-approved FSC-certified
paper carry the FSC logo. Our paper procurement policy can be
found at www.rbooks.co.uk/environment.

RANDOM HOUSE CHILDREN'S BOOKS
61–63 Uxbridge Road, London W5 5SA

www.**kids**at**randomhouse**.co.uk
www.**rbooks**.co.uk

Addresses for companies within The Random House Group Limited
can be found at: www.randomhouse.co.uk/offices.htm

THE RANDOM HOUSE GROUP Limited Reg. No. 954009

A CIP catalogue record for this book is available
from the British Library.

Printed and bound in China